NATURE 👓 WATCH

BOX TURTLES

Written and Photographed by
Lynn M. Stone

Lerner Publications Company • Minneapolis

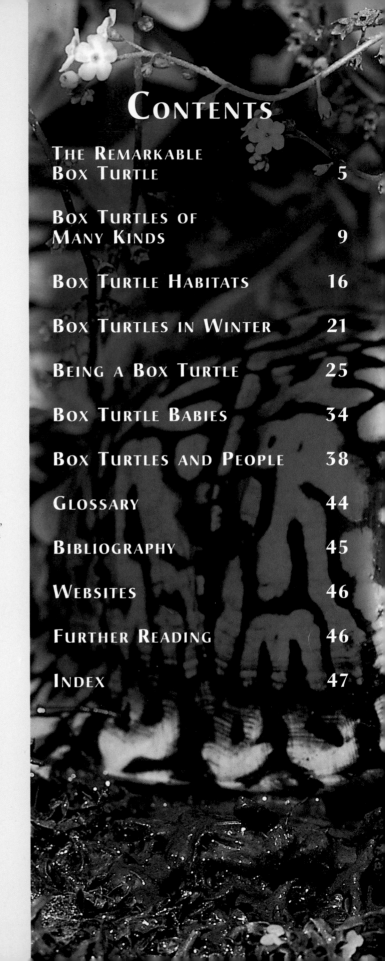

In memory of Ron Humbert, exemplary husband, father, and naturalist, a devoted friend to box turtles and a student of their lives. It was a privilege to share his company and joy of the natural world.

ACKNOWLEDGMENTS
In the preparation of this book and its photographs, I am especially indebted to Matt Finstrom and the Arizona-Sonora Desert Museum; to Jim Buskirk; and to the late Ron Humbert. Each generously contributed time, counsel, and a wealth of knowledge. I am also indebted to my wife Lynda, my daughter Brittany, and my faithful golden retriever, for their indulgence and patience during my efforts to bring this book to fruition.

All photographs used with the permission of © Lynn M. Stone, except: Illustration on p. 15 by © Laura Westlund/Independent Picture Service; © Patrick Bennett/CORBIS, p. 39; U.S. Fish and Wildlife Service, p. 40 (top).

Lerner Publications Company
A division of Lerner Publishing Group
241 First Avenue North
Minneapolis, MN 55401

Website address: www.lernerbooks.com

Library of Congress Cataloging-in-Publication Data

Stone, Lynn M.
  Box turtles / written and photographed by Lynn M. Stone.
    p.   cm. — (Nature watch)
  Includes bibliographical references and index.
  ISBN-13: 978–1–57505–869–6 (lib. bdg. : alk. paper)
  ISBN-10: 1–57505–869–3 (lib. bdg. : alk. paper)
  1. Box turtle—Juvenile literature. I. Title. II. Series: Nature watch (Minneapolis, Minn.)
  QL666.C547S76 2007
  597.92—dc22   200601286T7

Manufactured in the United States of America
1 2 3 4 5 6 – DP – 12 11 10 09 08 07

CONTENTS

THE REMARKABLE
BOX TURTLE   5

BOX TURTLES OF
MANY KINDS   9

BOX TURTLE HABITATS   16

BOX TURTLES IN WINTER   21

BEING A BOX TURTLE   25

BOX TURTLE BABIES   34

BOX TURTLES AND PEOPLE   38

GLOSSARY   44

BIBLIOGRAPHY   45

WEBSITES   46

FURTHER READING   46

INDEX   47

The eastern box turtle is at home in the woods.

THE REMARKABLE BOX TURTLE

MEETING A BOX TURTLE ON A WOODLAND TRAIL IS ONE OF nature's wonderful little surprises. It would seem much more reasonable to find a turtle in a pond or river. A turtle on a trail may seem out of place, but the turtle isn't lost. Box turtles like water for a good soak on a hot day, and they can swim. But nearly all box turtles spend most of their lives on dry land. They can be found in woodlands, deserts, prairies, pastures, and even vegetable gardens.

Box turtles are unusual turtles because they live on land. They're also unusual for the bright colors some of them show on their shells and skin. The top shells of the most colorful box turtles are patterned with dabs, streaks, or spots of yellow or orange. Colors on the turtle's under shell are often just as bold. A box turtle's head and legs can be colored red, like the three-toed box turtle shown above. Or they can be black, brown,

5

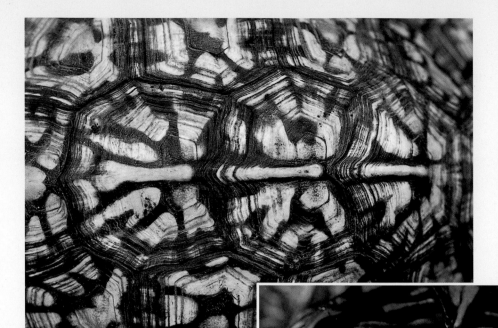

Top: The eastern box turtle's upper shell is part of its protective armor.

Right: This close-up of the lower shell of an ornate box turtle shows the hinge. This hinge makes it possible for a box turtle to close its shells completely.

white, orange, or yellow. A male Yucatán box turtle may have pink or blue flecks on its eyelids and throat. Adult male box turtles often have red eyes.

BOX TURTLE'S SHELLS

But it's neither box turtles' land-loving ways nor their crayon colors that make these little **reptiles** so unique. Rather, it is their shells. No other North American turtles have quite as remarkable a shell as box turtles do.

Like most turtles, a box turtle has two hard shells. Both are made of bones **fused** together. The upper shell is the **carapace**. The **plastron** is underneath. A box turtle's plastron has two sections hinged together by muscle. Each section can close upward, like a pickup truck's tailgate.

A frightened box turtle withdraws its feet, head, and neck into its shell, as many turtles do. But unlike other turtles, a box turtle can seal itself inside its shell, like a clam. A box turtle closes the front section of the plastron against the front edge of the carapace. It shuts the rear section of the plastron just as snugly against the back edge of the carapace. The turtle curls its long neck into an S shape and tucks it neatly away. (The turtle helps to make room for its head and neck by blowing the air out of its lungs.) The box turtle's soft body parts disappear inside the closed shell, leaving what looks more like a hard, domed box than a turtle!

Running from danger is not a good choice for a box turtle. Disappearing into its shell is.

EXTRA PROTECTION

A covering of **scutes** gives a box turtle shell extra protection and strength. Scutes are large scales of keratin. This is the same hornlike material as fingernails and hooves. Like shingles on a roof, the 38 scutes of the carapace and 12 of the plastron form protective layers on the shell surfaces.

This three-toed box turtle has closed its shell to protect it from enemies.

Scutes help a turtle hold moisture in its body, preventing dehydration, or drying out. They also contain the color pigment of a box turtle's shell. Since a box turtle doesn't shed its scutes, they grow along with the shell.

New scutes are shaped like low pyramids. They give the shells of young box turtles a finely chiseled appearance. As box turtles age, the sharp edges of the scutes wear smooth.

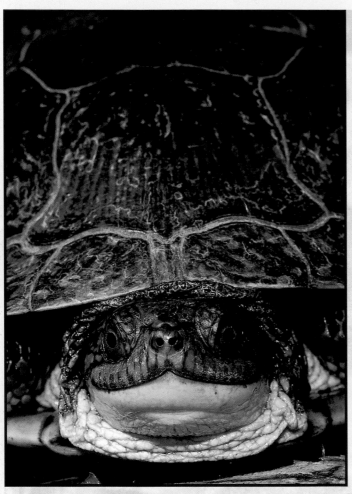

A Blanding's turtle cannot completely close its hinged plastron.

Other North American turtles, such as the Blanding's turtle and various musk turtles and mud turtles, also have hinged plastrons. But these turtles can only partially close their shells. The only turtles in the world that can completely escape into their shells are the North American box turtles and a group of unrelated Asian box turtles.

BOX TURTLES
OF MANY KINDS

ALL AMERICAN BOX TURTLES SHARE A SIMILAR BODY PLAN, but they do not all belong to the same **species.** There are four North American box turtle species: the eastern *(shown above)*, ornate, Coahuilan, and spotted. They share such features as a dome-shaped carapace and a hinged plastron. They all belong to a group of turtles that **herpetologists**, the scientists who study reptiles, call *Terrapene*. Scientists borrowed *Terrapene* from an Indian word meaning "turtle." Each box turtle species has a specific scientific name. For instance, *Terrapene carolina* is the name for the eastern box turtle.

Except for the Coahuilan box turtle that lives in water, North American box turtles have similar habits but different **habitats**, the types of places where they live. The box turtles of each region also differ some-what in size, shape, and color. In addition, they differ in ways that only a herpetologist would notice, such as certain features of their skull bones.

Herpetologists divide the four box turtle species into **subspecies**. Subspecies are groups within a species that are different, but not different enough to be entirely different species. Each box turtle subspecies lives, more or less, in a separate region. In fact, it is largely because populations of box turtles were separated that they evolved into subspecies. For example, rivers or mountains can prevent one group of animals from reaching others of the same kind. Over a long period of time, each group gradually changes in ways that suit its own special environment.

EASTERN BOX TURTLES

The eastern box turtle is the state reptile of North Carolina and Tennessee. It is the best known of the box turtles in the United States and Canada. There are six subspecies of the eastern box turtle: the Florida, the Mexican, the Yucatán, the Gulf Coast, the three-toed, and the turtle simply known as the eastern box turtle. The eastern box turtle is the colorful subspecies that lives in most of the eastern United States and southern Ontario. Scientists know it as *Terrapene carolina carolina*. The Florida box turtle lives throughout Florida. It has a particularly high carapace, usually streaked with yellow rays.

Above: **The Gulf Coast box turtle is found in the coastal states of the Gulf of Mexico.**
Right: **The Florida box turtle, found only in Florida, is a subspecies of the eastern box turtle.**

Three-toed box turtles live in the south central United States. Most of them have three toes on their back feet.

The Gulf Coast box turtle, the largest of all box turtles, is found on the Florida Panhandle and along the upper Gulf Coast. The largest box turtle on record had a carapace 8.6 inches (22 cm) from the front edge to the back edge.

The three-toed subspecies of the eastern box turtle lives in the central United States from Texas north into Missouri. Most three-toed box turtles—although not all—have three clawed toes on each hind foot. Other box turtles—and the occasional three-toed—have four clawed toes on their hind feet. All box turtles, including the three-toed, have four clawed front toes.

The Mexican and Yucatán subspecies of the eastern box turtle live in Mexico. Herpetologists know almost nothing about the life histories of these turtles in the wild because they have not been carefully studied.

Above and right: The Mexican and Yucatán box turtle's habits remain a mystery to scientists.

Above: The small ornate box turtle of the midwestern prairies can outrace the eastern box turtle.

The desert box turtle lives in the American Southwest and Mexico.

Ornate box turtles walk more quickly than eastern box turtles. Perhaps it is because they generally live in more open country and have fewer hiding places. An eastern box turtle at top speed would take about 20 minutes to travel the length of a football field from one goal line to the other. An ornate box turtle could go the same distance in about 7 minutes.

ORNATE BOX TURTLES

Ornate box turtles are typically smaller and have more rounded carapaces than eastern box turtles. The state reptile of Kansas, the ornate box turtle was named for the ornate, or fancy, yellow streaks on its dark carapace. The easternmost subspecies is known as the ornate box turtle. It lives largely in the grasslands of the West and Midwest, including the states of Wisconsin, Illinois, and Indiana. The western subspecies of the ornate box turtle is called the desert, or western, box turtle. It lives in the American Southwest and in the states of Sonora and Chihuahua in Mexico. As they age, the carapaces of some desert box turtles change from dark brown with yellow streaks to a uniform brownish or yellowish.

13

OTHER SPECIES

The third species of box turtle is Mexico's spotted box turtle. Scientists know little about its life history. They recognize two subspecies, the northern and southern. When these turtles are studied more closely, scientists may decide that all spotted turtles belong to a single species.

The fourth species of box turtle is the Coahuilan. This **endangered** species is the most unusual box turtle because it lives in water, or is **aquatic.** It is often called the aquatic box turtle. It has been found only in the Cuatro Ciénegas, a low, wet area within Mexico's Chihuahuan Desert. The Coahuilan box turtle spends most of its life in the ponds and marshes of this area. The Coahuilan box turtle has a more stream-lined shell than its land-loving cousins. The flatter dome of its carapace helps a Coahuilan box turtle swim with less water resistance.

Left: Scientists know very little about the spotted box turtle.
Below: The Coahuilan box turtle lives in the wetlands of Mexico's Chihuahuan Desert.

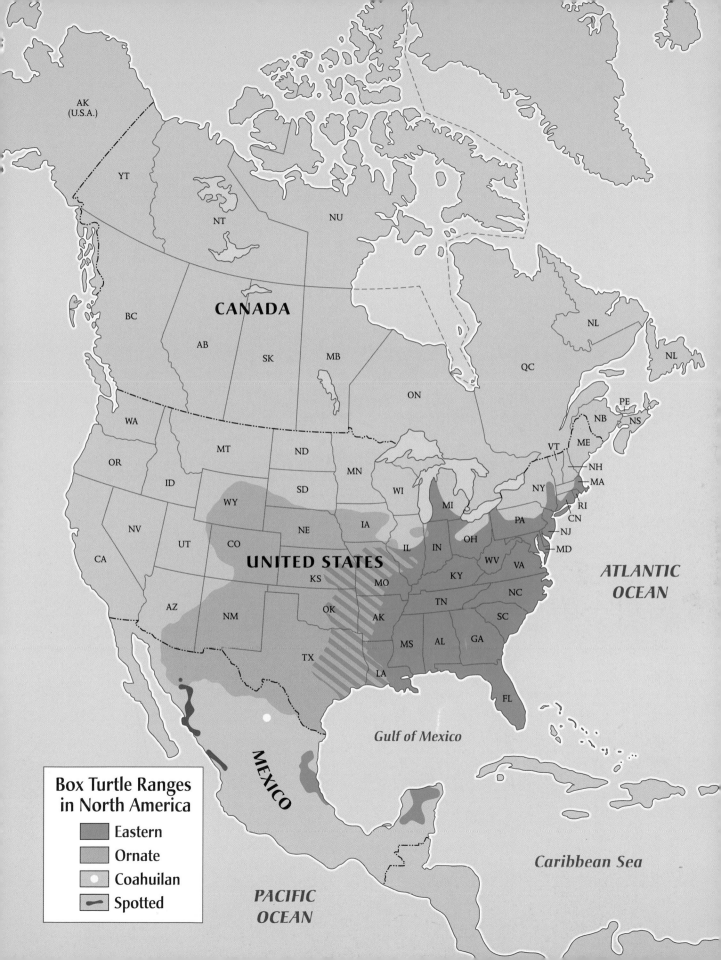

AK
(U.S.A.)

YT

NT

NU

CANADA

BC

AB

SK

MB

ON

QC

NL

NL

PE

NB

NS

WA

MT

ND

MN

VT

ME

OR

ID

SD

WI

NH

NY

MA

WY

MI

PA

RI

CN

NV

NE

IA

IL

IN

OH

WV

NJ

MD

CA

UT

CO

UNITED STATES

KS

MO

KY

VA

ATLANTIC
OCEAN

AZ

NM

OK

AK

TN

NC

SC

TX

MS

AL

GA

LA

FL

Gulf of Mexico

MEXICO

Caribbean Sea

PACIFIC
OCEAN

Box Turtle Ranges in North America

- Eastern
- Ornate
- Coahuilan
- Spotted

Box Turtle
Habitats

Most box turtles live in a variety of habitats. The various subspecies of eastern box turtles, for example, can be found in many different woodland habitats filled with oak, hickory, pine, birch, elm, maple, or other trees. The Florida subspecies can be found in the saw grass marshes of the Florida Everglades, in woodlands, and even near seashores. Some eastern box turtles live at sea level. Others amble through mountain forests 4,000 feet (1,200 m) above sea level.

Farther west, ornate and desert box turtles *(shown above)* live in a variety of prairie and desert grasslands. At the edges of the prairies, ornate box turtles often wander into forest groves to cool off. Desert box turtles have been found on pine-and-forested slopes of the American Southwest at more than 7,000 feet (2,134 m) above sea level.

An ornate box turtle ambles among the prairie flowers called blazing stars. A painted lady butterfly collects nectar from the flower blossoms.

HABITATS IN SEASON

Box turtles often travel from one habitat to another. They don't travel far in human terms, but neither do they stay on a single, tiny patch of ground. Because box turtles don't travel long distances, they seem to like environments in which different little habitats are near one another. A box turtle can then visit two or more different habitats

in a day. It can rest in a sunny place, such as a garden, and later move to the cool air of a forest.

Box turtles also seem to favor certain habitats according to the season. They show up in open lands more commonly in spring. In warm summer weather, the turtles often shift their activity to woodlands or the soggy bottomlands along rivers. These habitats have cooling shelters of fallen leaves and hollows under stumps and logs. They also have patches of open ground that attract warm pools of sunlight.

The three-toed box turtle encounters the large prairie flower in its habitat.

An eastern box turtle suns itself on a patch of moss.

COLD-BLOODED TURTLES

Having a cozy spot to warm up or cool down is a matter of life and death for a box turtle. As a reptile, a box turtle is a **cold-blooded** animal. The term *cold-blooded* describes an animal whose body temperature is controlled by the temperature of the air or water around it. Box turtles have cold blood when the air is cold. But they also have relatively warm blood when they bask in sunlight. In contrast, warm-blooded birds and mammals maintain a steady body temperature. It doesn't depend on the surrounding air or water temperature.

For a box turtle to remain active, it must keep a safe and comfortable body temperature. If a box turtle's body temperature rises above 105.8°F (41°C), the turtle will pant like a dog. Panting is an effort to release heat through the throat and mouth. If a box turtle's body temperature continues to rise, the turtle will die.

In hot weather box turtles, like this eastern, will cool off in a pond or brook.

The best temperature level of a box turtle depends upon the species and even the location of the species. Herpetologists have learned, for example, that ornate box turtles in Wisconsin maintain a lower body temperature than ornate box turtles in Kansas, which is farther south.

Intense heat or a sudden cold snap can kill a box turtle, so the animal always needs places where it can find shelter from extreme weather. During hot, dry weather, box turtles often leave their land habitats and enter cool brooks or ponds for short periods.

FORMS

Another retreat for a box turtle in almost all of its land habitats is called a **form.** A form is a shallow depression in leaf litter, grass, or loose soil. A box turtle scratches out the form with its clawed front feet. Then it wiggles into the form, using its shell to widen the little hollow. A box turtle can be somewhat hidden in its form. A form also offers some shade on hot days and refuge from wind on colder days.

A box turtle may have several forms. It may visit many of them during one day's travels. A turtle doesn't defend its form, though, so unoccupied forms may be used by any box turtle that wanders by. A box turtle uses a form in the daytime whenever it senses the need. It also uses a form at night, when box turtles are seldom active.

This ornate box turtle is about ready to seek shelter in the form it dug for itself.

Box Turtles in Winter

Box turtles in the north are not active when the air turns cold. The cold air causes the box turtle's body temperature to drop. With the drop in body temperature, a box turtle becomes increasingly sluggish, like an aging battery. When autumn's frosty weather arrives, box turtles seek a place to spend the winter. Most box turtles dig a depression in the earth. Eastern box turtles *(shown above)* dig rather shallow depressions. They are usually no more than 4 inches (10 cm) deep. An eastern box turtle often leaves the top of its shell exposed. Ornate box turtles usually dig deeper. Herpetologists have found ornate box turtles in Wisconsin, at the most northern part of their range, at an average of about 3 feet (1 m) below ground.

Box turtles pick other places to overwinter too—hillsides, stump holes, and even the muddy bottom of ponds. They also overwinter in the burrows of mammals such as kangaroo rats. Wherever a box turtle spends the cold months, it finds more warmth than if it had been exposed to winter air. Even the shallow pits that eastern box turtles dig are much warmer than the air above them.

The Florida box turtle *(at right)* doesn't need to seek shelter in winter, but it does become less active in cool weather.

The eastern box turtle needs to find shelter from winter temperatures.

These two turtles—an eastern box turtle *(left)* and a three-toed turtle—are in torpor. They were uncovered for this photograph.

TORPOR

Inside their forms or burrows, box turtles in the North, like many other reptiles, enter a state of complete inactivity in winter. This is called **torpor**.

Box turtles become torpid as temperatures drop to freezing, usually by October. Their body functions slow down dramatically. Other severe weather conditions can also cause torpor. In a long summer drought, box turtles sometimes enter a torpid state in the mud of ponds.

In the coldest conditions, a box turtle's heart may stop and more than half its body moisture can turn to ice. If the extreme cold doesn't last for more than a day or two, however, the box turtle can recover. Scientists do not yet understand how this is possible.

Torpid turtles are often described as hibernating. But torpor is somewhat different from **hibernation**. Certain mammals, such as woodchucks, hibernate. Their body functions slow down too. But the body of a hibernating mammal will eventually warm up on its own.

Then the animal will emerge from hibernation in the spring. Box turtles leave their torpid state only when spring warms the air or when rainfall ends a period of drought. Early warm spells sometimes cause box turtles to become active too soon. A sudden return of winter temperatures can kill them.

An Eastern box turtle reemerges from torpor in the warmth of spring.

BEING A
BOX TURTLE

BOX TURTLES, SUCH AS THE GULF COAST BOX TURTLE, ABOVE, are slow-moving by nature. They give the appearance of leading calm and unhurried lives. But in their own way, they are busy and alert. After all, their survival depends upon their ability to avoid danger and find food, water, shelter, and mates.

By human standards, a box turtle lives in a very small corner of the world. This little neighborhood is called a **home range.** A box turtle's home range is typically between 2 and 5 acres (0.8 to 2.0 hectares). Most box turtles stay in or near this range throughout their lives. Others wander beyond the home range occasionally when looking for a site to escape winter or drought or a place to rest. Some box turtles apparently travel back and forth between two home ranges. A few—especially certain males—wander more widely. Some box turtles may wander over

The ornate box turtle's home range is on the prairie.

several miles without ever establishing a home range.

Box turtles can return to familiar places because, like people, they learn to recognize objects in their environment, such as rocks, fences, stumps, trees, and turtle trails. They also have a strong homing instinct. This allows them to find their way back home after traveling some distance. The homing instinct is apparently aided by a box turtle's ability to use the position of the sun as a guide. In darkness or on cloudy days, the box turtle's homing instincts are useless.

This eastern box turtle navigates over fallen branches to return to its home range.

Box turtles in much of the southern United States are active year-round. In the north, box turtles are generally active from March or April into October or November.

A box turtle can't do anything until its body warms up. In spring or fall, a box turtle will not leave the form where it spent the night until the sun is high enough to warm the air. But the same turtle may begin to move at dawn on a warm summer morning.

TURTLES TOGETHER

Box turtles aren't particularly social. But they often cross paths and generally seem to tolerate one another. One box turtle's home range may be part of another box turtle's home range, making them neighbors. A bonanza of food, such as a fallen crop of ripe berries, may lure several box turtles to the same bush. During warm weather, many box turtles may share a pool. And several box turtles may overwinter close to one another.

Sometimes box turtles fight. Fighting box turtles bite and push one another. A fight ends when one turtle walks away from the combat. Scientists aren't sure how often wild box turtles fight or for what reasons. Males probably fight over female box turtles. Perhaps an occasional box turtle will fight to keep a strange box turtle out of its home range. Captive box turtles fight over food or over mates. They may fight to decide which is most dominant. It may be that wild box turtles fight for exactly the same reasons.

Two Yucatán box turtles cross paths.

Box turtles in the south, such as this Florida box turtle, are active in their home range year-round.

Left: A three-toed box turtle devours an earthworm.
Below: Mushrooms are a favorite food of box turtles, including this young eastern box turtle.

TURTLE FOODS

On any given day, a box turtle may leave its form to **forage**, or search, for food. A box turtle doesn't have to eat every day, but it probably eats whenever it has the chance, especially in the late spring and into midsummer. That's when food is most plentiful.

Box turtles are **omnivores**. Like people, they eat both plant and animal matter. But unlike people, box turtles will eat almost anything. They eat many kinds of mushrooms, including some whose **toxins** would send a human to a hospital.

Box turtles also eat leaves, grasses, berries, roots, fruits, and vegetables.

Box turtles like flesh too, living or dead. All the box turtle species and subspecies that have been studied hunt small, moving **prey**. Earthworms, snails, slugs, millipedes, and insects are at the top of their list. Box turtles can be sur-prisingly quick when snapping at live prey. Ornate box turtles even chase grasshoppers.

With their broad tastes, box turtles can usually find food easily. But they sometimes have to work for their meals

Above: **Other eastern box turtles may join this one to take advantage of the ripe berries.**

by scratching through leaf litter and dung piles for bugs and other little creatures. Many box turtle species hunt on land. But Coahuilan box turtles, like other aquatic turtles, do most of their hunting in ponds and marshes.

Box turtles have hard, sharp-edged jaws. They pull food apart with their jaws while holding it firmly with their front feet.

They have no teeth, so they can't chew. They swallow pieces of food whole.

A box turtle may be active for reasons besides foraging. The turtle may be moving to another form or to some location where it can change its body temperature. The turtle may just need a water break. Box turtles also move about to find mates and nesting sites.

Above: **This Mexican box turtle—and all other box turtles too—pull food apart with their sharp jaws and swallow it whole.**
Inset: **Coahuilan box turtles hunt for food in water.**

The male and a female eastern box turtles may have used their senses to find one another. The male is the one with the red eyes.

BOX TURTLE SENSES

Box turtles find food mainly by seeing it. Scientists aren't sure how sharp box turtles' vision is, but a box turtle sees well enough to recognize sudden drop-offs, obstacles on its path, and the movements of prey. And they apparently respond to colors well enough to know a ripe berry from a green one.

Box turtles can hear, but it is not known whether they hear in the manner that people do. They may just feel sound vibrations. They don't seem to respond to humans who yell at them, but that does not mean that they are deaf.

A box turtle's sense of smell is a bit of a mystery as well. Box turtles touch their snouts to the ground as if smelling. But herpetologists do not know for sure if box turtles really smell anything. Herpetologists are fairly sure, though, that box turtles don't have the keen smelling sense of snakes and lizards. Whether a box turtle has a sense of taste is another mystery to human observers.

Box Turtle
Babies

Box turtles have to find one another to produce more of their kind. They may do it strictly by dumb luck, or scent may play a role—assuming they have a sense of smell.

Most box turtle matings occur in April and May, although they can mate at any time during their active seasons. A female and male box turtle may mate almost immediately after meeting, or they may engage in an hour or several hours of courtship. A courting male eastern box turtle will typically bite the female's shell, as in the photo above. The male may also push the female or drag her toward him. After mating, each turtle goes its own way.

Female box turtles usually lay their eggs in June or July. Eastern box turtles typically lay 4 to 6 eggs, but box turtles may lay just 1 egg or as many as 11. Each group of eggs is called a **clutch.** Some box turtles lay two or more clutches each year.

The female turtle lays her eggs in a hole that she digs with her hind feet. She drops the eggs from the **ovipositor** beneath the base of her tail. Egg-laying takes anywhere from 10 to about 25 minutes. After the eggs are laid, the box turtle uses her hind feet to refill the nest hole with soil. Then she pushes pebbles or leaves over the nest site to hide it. After she has buried her eggs, she leaves. The box turtle's mothering duties are over.

Box turtle eggs are at high risk. A nest may be flooded, drowning the babies inside the eggs. It may be raided by a predator, such as a raccoon or a fox, that smells the eggs or the female box turtle's scent. Ants can destroy box turtle eggs. Snakes sometimes grab and eat the eggs as the box turtle lays them.

The eggs are buried about 60 days. During this time, the baby turtles grow and develop within the soft shells.

There are six eastern box turtle eggs in this uncovered nest.

Each baby has a **yolk sac** attached to its body. The yolk provides food for the growing turtle.

Weather helps determine exactly how long the eggs **incubate**. Warm weather or a sunny nest site helps turtles to develop faster. Baby box turtles usually hatch in August or September.

HATCHING

Each baby turtle has a tiny growth called a **caruncle**, or egg tooth, on its snout. Over a period of several hours or even days, a hatchling turtle in its egg uses the caruncle to break open the eggshell. Meanwhile, the yolk continues to feed the baby. The yolk even nourishes the hatchling for its first few days out of the egg. The turtle's body normally absorbs the yolk sac within a week. For baby box turtles in northern regions, the yolk is the hatchling's nourishment for its torpid period during the coming winter.

Young box turtles must spend their early months and years well hidden. A young box turtle's shell is fairly soft. It hardens with age. The dull, earth colors of the baby turtles' soft, silver dollar-sized shells help conceal them. Otherwise, even more of them would be snacks for raccoons, foxes, badgers, coyotes, ravens, vultures, snakes, and many other **predators**.

By the age of 7 or 8 years, box turtles have reached most of their adult size. Some growth may continue until the animals are about 20. Many box turtles are old enough to seek mates by the age of 5. Others are 7 or 8 before they **reproduce**.

A baby box turtle uses its egg tooth to break out of its shell.

Each hatchling box turtle still has an attached yolk sac to feed it for the first few days.

This eastern box turtle hatchling still has a soft shell and must remain hidden from predators.

Box Turtle Enemies

Adult box turtles have few natural enemies, other than disease, fire, sudden shifts in weather, and a few **parasites**, such as mites, ticks, flies, and various worms. The shells of the adults are too hard for almost any predator to crush in its jaws. But scientists have found box turtles with parts of their feet missing. This suggests that they sometimes try to escape a predator by hustling away rather than withdrawing into the armor of their shells.

Turtles have a reputation for living long lives, but it is difficult to determine the true age of a turtle. Records of captive turtles do not necessarily reflect how long wild turtles might live. Still, it is likely that box turtles often reach the age of 50 and perhaps 100.

The shell of this juvenile ornate box turtle has hardened, but the turtle still has to watch for predators.

Box Turtles
and People

Many peoples of North America have had a close relationship with box turtles. Native American sites more than 5,000 years old have revealed box turtle bones, which were probably leftovers from ancient feasts. More recent native people, including the Sioux and Kiowa, also have a tradition of eating box turtles.

Beginning perhaps 2,000 years ago, some Native American groups began using box turtle shells in ceremonies. Shells filled with pebbles were used for rattles. Shells were also crafted into bowls and ornaments. Cherokees, Senecas, and several other Native American groups still use box turtle rattles, such as this Cherokee rattle (*shown above*), in their stomp dances.

Box turtles may have had ceremonial importance too among the Mayans on the Yucatán Peninsula of Mexico. Mayans built the House of Turtles about 1,200 years ago. Some of the carvings on that building seem to represent Yucatán box turtles.

THREATS

Box turtles remain fairly common in some areas. In other places, they have become rare. Highway traffic takes a huge toll on them. But the single greatest threat to box turtles is the ongoing loss of their habitats to farms, new highways, subdivisions, and shopping malls.

Box turtle populations have also suffered at the hands of collectors. Professional collectors sent thousands of live American box turtles to Europe, Japan, and Hong Kong in the early 1990s for sale as pets. New laws have stopped the widespread export of box turtles, but trade—legal and illegal—in wild box turtles continues.

Cold and crusty, turtles have never caught the public's fancy the way that animals with fur and feathers have. This makes it difficult to convince governments

Many box turtles are killed on highways as they slowly make their way across.

Above: **Fish and Wildlife Service biologists study eastern box turtles. The numbers of these turtles are falling because of loss of habitat and capture by turtle collectors.**
Inset: **The endangered Coahuilan box turtle is protected in the United States.**

to pass tough turtle protection laws. The only box turtle that receives complete protection from the U.S. government is the endangered Coahuilan box turtle—and it lives in Mexico. Some states, including Michigan, Massachusetts, and Wisconsin, have passed tough laws regarding the capture, sale, and possession of box turtles.

Unfortunately, state laws contain many loopholes. Illinois, for example, bars the sale of "wild-caught native species." You cannot sell eastern or ornate box turtles in Illinois if they were caught there. But it is legal in Illinois to sell the three-toed box turtles you picked up in Missouri, although it is not legal to sell those same turtles in Missouri.

Protective laws are hard to enforce, and box turtles are hard to resist. They do not have quite the charm of pup- pies, but they can be quite attractive and charmingly shy. Only the occasion- al box turtle—usually an ornate—is likely to resist its captor by biting.

Once discovered, a box turtle has no

Box turtles have their own special appeal and sometimes become pets.

In some parts of North America, people call box turtles terrapins or tortoises. Terrapin is a nickname for many kinds of turtles. True tortoises are turtles that live on land and have thick, blunt, elephant-like hind feet. Four species of true tortoises live in North America: the gopher tortoise of the Southeast, the Texas tortoise of southern Texas, the desert tortoise *(shown here)* of the Southwest, and the endangered Bolson tortoise of Mexico.

means to escape someone bent on possessing it. The turtle can only retreat into its shell. As a result, people often pick up these harmless creatures to take home for pets.

Most people don't realize they may be breaking a state law by keeping a box turtle. But beyond the legal issue, very few people have the living space or the knowledge to take proper care of a box turtle. Box turtles are wild animals, and they are best left in the wild exactly where they were found.

The box turtle is one of nature's unique creations and a natural part of North America's wetlands, prairies, and forests. Our efforts to keep those places wild will help keep these fascinating little reptiles with the boxy shells out and about for centuries to come.

The unique box turtle will wander freely as long as we protect its natural habitats from destruction.

GLOSSARY

aquatic: living or occurring in water

carapace: a turtle's upper shell

caruncle: a growth on a turtle hatchling's snout. It is used to break open its egg.

clutch: the group of eggs laid in the nest

cold-blooded: unable to control body temperature

endangered: at risk of disappearing forever

forage: to search for food

form: a shallow hole in the ground made by a turtle for protection from weather

fused: to be joined together

habitats: the kinds of environments in which animals normally live

herpetologists: scientists who study reptiles

hibernation: spending the winter in a sleeplike state in which body systems slow dramatically

home range: the area that a box turtle lives in, where it finds food and shelter

incubate: to keep eggs protected and at the proper temperature until they hatch

omnivores: animals that eat both plants and other animals

ovipositor: the organ of the female turtle that is used to lay eggs

parasites: animals that live in or on other animals and depend on them for food

plastron: the part of the shell under a turtle's body

predators: animals that hunt other animals

prey: animals that are food for hunting animals

reproduce: to mate to produce young

reptiles: cold-blooded animals that lay eggs and that have skin covered with scales. They include lizards, snakes, turtles, and crocodiles.

scutes: hornlike scales on a turtle's shell

species: a kind of animal or plant. Members of the same species can mate and reproduce.

subspecies: groups within a species that are different but not different enough to be a distinct species. Different subspecies often live in different areas.

torpor: a state in which bodily functions slow down. It is caused by cold weather or drought.

toxins: poisons

yolk sac: a sac attached to a baby turtle that contains food

BIBLIOGRAPHY

Anderson, Paul. *The Reptiles of Missouri*. Columbia: University of Missouri Press, 1965.

Bailey, Joseph R., Julian R. Harrison, Bernard S. Martof, and William M. Palmer. *Amphibians and Reptiles of the Carolinas and Virginia*. Chapel Hill: University of North Carolina Press, 1980.

Brandon, Ronald A., Edward O. Moll, and Christopher A. Phillips. *Field Guide to Amphibians and Reptiles of Illinois*. Champaign: Illinois Natural History Survey, 1999.

Carr, Archie, and Coleman J. Goin. *Guide to the Reptiles, Amphibians, and Fresh-Water Fishes of Florida*. Gainesville: University of Florida Press, 1955.

Censky, Ellen J., Arthur C. Hulse, and C. J. McCoy. *Amphibians and Reptiles of Pennsylvania and the Northeast*. Ithaca, NY: Cornell University Press, 2001.

Conant, Roger. *A Field Guide to Reptiles and Amphibians of Eastern and Central North America*. 2nd ed. Boston: Houghton Mifflin Company, 1975.

Dodd, Kenneth C., Jr. *North American Box Turtles: A Natural History*. Norman: University of Oklahoma Press, 2001.

Ernst, Carl H., Jeffrey E. Lovich, and Roger W. Barbour. *Turtles of the United States and Canada*. Washington, DC: Smithsonian Institution Press, 1994.

Ernst, Carl H., and Roger W. Barbour. T*urtles of the World*. Washington, DC: Smithsonian Institution Press, 1989.

Harding, James H. *Amphibians and Reptiles of the Great Lakes Region*. Ann Arbor: University of Michigan Press, 1997.

Johnson, Tom R. *The Amphibians and Reptiles of Missouri*. Jefferson City: Missouri Department of Conservation, 1992.

Legler, John M. *Natural History of the Ornate Box Turtle, Terrapene ornate ornate Agassiz*. Lawrence: University of Kansas Press, 1960.

Shaffer, Larry L. *Pennsylvania Amphibians and Reptiles*. Harrisburg: Pennsylvania Fish Commission, Bureau of Education and Information, 1991.

Smith, Philip W. *The Amphibians and Reptiles of Illinois*. Urbana: Survey Division, Illinois Department of Registration and Education, 1961.

Stebbins, Robert C. *A Field Guide to Western Reptiles and Amphibians*. Boston: Houghton Mifflin Company, 1966.

Tyning, Thomas F., ed. *Status and Conservation of Turtles of the Northeastern United States*. Lincoln: Massachusetts Audubon Society, 1997.

WEBSITES

Illinois Natural History Survey
   http://www.inhs.uiuc.edu.
   This site includes an Illinois Natural History Survey report on the eastern box turtle.
Indiana Turtle Care
   http://www.pogospals.com
   The site contains information on box turtles of all sorts. It also includes articles about how to care for box turtles and on turtle rehabilitation and conservation.
Missouri's Two Box Turtles
   www.mdc.mo.gov/nathis/herpetol/boxturtles
   This is an online version of an article with photos from *Conservationist* magazine. It gives the natural histories of the three-toed and ornate box turtles.

FURTHER READING

George, William T. *Box Turtle at Long Pond.* New York: HarperCollins, 1989.
   Hirschi, Ron. *Turtle's Day.* New York: Penguin, 1994.
MacMillan, Dianne *Life in a Deciduous Forest.* Minneapolis: Twenty-First Century Books, 2003.
Patent, Dorothy Hushow. *Life in a Desert.* Minneapolis: Twenty-First Century Books, 2003.
Patent, Dorothy Hushow. *Life in a Grassland.* Minneapolis: Twenty-First Century Books, 2003.

INDEX

body temperature, 18, 21, 23, 28

clutch, 34
Coahuilan box turtle, 9, 14, 32, 40
cold-blooded, 18

defense mechanism, 6, 7, 37, 42
desert box turtles (western box turtles), 13, 16

eastern box turtle (species), 5–8, 10, 12, 15–25, 28, 30–39, 41, 42
eastern box turtles, 6, 9, 10, 13, 16, 18, 19, 21, 22, 24, 27, 30, 31, 33–37, 40
eggs, 30, 34–36
endangered, 14, 40

fighting, 28
Florida box turtles, 10, 16, 22, 29
food, 30–33
form, 20, 23, 28

Gulf Coast box turtles, 10, 25

habitat, 5, 9, 16, 17, 20, 39, 40
herpetologist, 9, 10, 12, 20, 21, 33
hibernation, 23, 24
home range, 25–28
homing instinct, 27

life span, 37

mating, 34
Mexican box turtles, 10, 12, 32
Mexican spotted box turtle, 9, 14

Native Americans, 38–39
nests, 25, 32, 35

omnivores, 30
ornate box turtle (subspecies), 13, 16, 17, 20, 26, 37, 40, 41, 43
ornate box turtles (species), 6, 9, 13, 15, 21, 31

protective laws, 40–41

shell, 5–8, 14, 36, 37, 38; carapace, 6–7, 9–10, 12, 13, 14; plastron, 6–9; scutes, 7, 8
social, 28
speed, 13, 25

terrapins, 42
threats, 39–42
three-toed box turtles, 5, 7, 10, 11, 12, 17, 23, 30, 40
toes, 12
torpor, 23, 24, 36
tortoise, 42

Yucatán box turtle, 6, 10, 12, 28, 39

ABOUT THE AUTHOR

Lynn M. Stone is an author and wildlife photographer who has written more than 400 books for young readers about wildlife and natural history. Stone enjoys fishing and travel and, of course, photographing wildlife. He is a former teacher and lives with his family in Saint Charles, Illinois.